The early Part-songs
1890-1891

for SATB with divisions

Edward Elgar

Order No: NOV 070433R

NOVELLO PUBLISHING LIMITED

CONTENTS

O HAPPY EYES

PART-SONG FOR S.A.T.B.

THE WORDS WRITTEN BY C. ALICE ELGAR

THE MUSIC COMPOSED BY

EDWARD ELGAR.

(Op. 18, No. 1.)

TO C.A.E.

LOVE

PART-SONG FOR S.A.T.B.

THE WORDS WRITTEN BY ARTHUR MAQUARIE

THE MUSIC COMPOSED BY

EDWARD ELGAR.

(Op. 18, No. 2.)

8

10

Thus I looked to heav'n a - gain, Yearn - ing up with

Thus I looked to heav'n a - gain, Yearn - ing,

Thus I looked to heav'n a - gain, Yearn - ing up with

Thus I looked to heav'n a - gain, Yearn - ing

ea - ger, ea - ger eyes, As

yearn - ing, yearn - ing up with ea - ger eyes, As

ea - ger eyes, yearn - ing up with ea - ger eyes, As

up with ea - ger eyes, As

Come 1ma, ma più lento.

bright - - er glow, Let me ev - er gaze . .
bright - er . . glow, Let me ev - er gaze on
bright - er glow, Let me ev - er gaze on
bright - er . . glow, Let me ev - er gaze . . .

. . . . on thee, ... Lest I lose warm
thee, . . gaze on thee, . . Lest I lose warm
thee, . . gaze on thee, . . Lest I lose warm
. . . . . on thee. Lest I lose warm

MY LOVE DWELT IN A NORTHERN LAND

ROMANCE FOR S.A.T.B

THE WORDS WRITTEN BY ANDREW LANG*

THE MUSIC COMPOSED BY

EDWARD ELGAR.

* From *The Century Magazine*

* The passages of vocal accompaniment to be sung as softly and smoothly as posssible and without accent

18

20

Più lento
a tempo

love is green, ... His heart is cold-er than the clay,

grass a-bove my love is green, His heart is cold-er than the clay,

grass a-bove my love is green, His heart is cold, cold - er than the

grass a-bove my love is green, His heart is cold-er than the clay, ...

cold - er, cold - er than the clay. ...

cold - - er than the clay, cold - - er than the clay. ...

clay, his heart .. is cold - er, cold - er than the clay. ...

... than the clay. ...

SPANISH SERENADE
(STARS OF THE SUMMER NIGHT!)

FOR CHORUS (S.A.T.B.) AND ORCHESTRA

THE WORDS FROM LONGFELLOW'S "SPANISH STUDENT"

THE MUSIC COMPOSED BY

EDWARD ELGAR.

(OP. 23.)

(A street in Madrid. Enter CHISPA, followed by musicians, with a bagpipe, guitars, and other instruments.)

Full score and orchestral parts may be had of the Publishers.

The Choral Music of

Edward Elgar

The Apostles
oratorio for SATBB soli, chorus & orchestra.

Caractacus
cantata for STBarB soli, chorus & orchestra.

The Dream of Gerontius
oratorio for M-S TB soli, chorus & orchestra.

The Early Part Songs (1890 – 1891)
for SATB with divisions.

Five Unaccompanied Part-Songs opus 71, 72 & 73
for SATB with divisions.

Four Latin Motets
for SATB & organ.

Four Unaccompanied Part-Songs opus 53
for SATB with divisions.

From the Greek Anthology
five unaccompanied part-songs for TTBB.

Give Unto the Lord (Psalm 29)
for chorus & orchestra.

Great is the Lord
for SATB chorus & organ or orchestra.

The Kingdom
oratorio for SATB soli, chorus & orchestra.

The Later Part-Songs (1902 – 1925)
for unaccompanied SATB with divisions.

The Light of Life (Lux Christi)
oratorio for SATBar soli, chorus & orchestra.

The Music Makers
ode for Contralto solo, chorus & orchestra.

Seven Anthems
for SATB (one for SA).

The Spirit of England
for S or T solo, chorus & orchestra.

Te Deum & Benedictus in F
for SATB chorus, orchestra & organ.

Three Unaccompanied Part-Songs
for SATB with divisions.